101 Bright Bulletin Board Ideas

Copyright 1991 by Glenda Lee

Q QUALITY PUBLICATIONS
P.O. BOX 7385
FT. WORTH, TX 76111

ISBN: 0-89137-626-7

Don't run out of time...

TO LATE St.

Study Gods word

"You were running well; who hindered you from obeying the truth?"
—*Galatians 5:7*

1

"A FRIEND LOVES AT ALL TIMES,"

—Proverbs 17:17

Don't Clown around in Bible Class

"and there must be no filthiness and silly talk, or coarse jesting, which are not fitting, but rather giving of thanks."

—*Ephesians 5:4*

"Keep my commandments and live, and my teaching as the apple of your eye."

—*Proverbs 7:2*

"Keep me as the apple of the eye;"

—*Psalms 17:8*

The best book to read... The BIBLE

"Be diligent to present yourself approved to God as a workman who does not need to be ashamed, handling accurately the word of truth."

—2 Timothy 2:15

Bless be the tie that binds

"And do not forsake the teaching of your mother; Bind them continually on your heart; Tie them around your neck."

—*Proverbs 6:20,21*

6

"and to know the love of Christ which surpasses knowledge, that you may be filled up to all the fulness of God."

—*Ephesians 3:19*

fill my cup ...

let it overflow with ... Gods love

"for you are all sons of light and sons of day. . ."
—*1 Thessalonians 5:5*

Let Other's see the "SON" shining in you!

"But now abide faith, hope, love, these three; but the greatest of these is Love."

—*1 Corinthians 13:13*

Rooted & grounded

in God's Love

"so that Christ may dwell in your hearts through faith; and that you, being rooted and grounded in love, may be able to comprehend with all the saints what is the breadth and length and height and depth."

—*Ephesians 3:17,18*

"Do all things without grumbling or disputing."

—*Philippians 2:14*

Which door will you choose?

"I have come as light into the world, that everyone who believes in Me may not remain in darkness."

—John 12:46

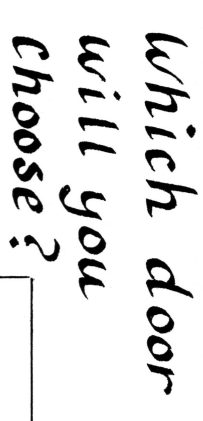

DARKNESS of SIN

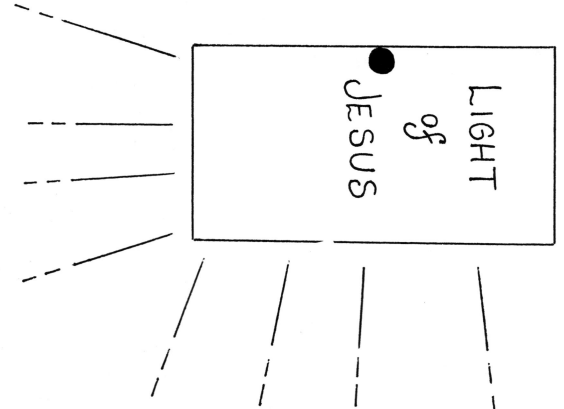

LIGHT of JESUS

" 'You shall love your neighbor as yourself.' "

—Matthew 22:39

Our Bible Class in Blooming with God's love!

"The one who does not love does not know God, for God is love."

—*1 John 4:8*

"Let each one do just as he has purposed in his heart; not grudgingly or under compulsion; for God loves a cheerful giver."

—*2 Corinthians 9:7*

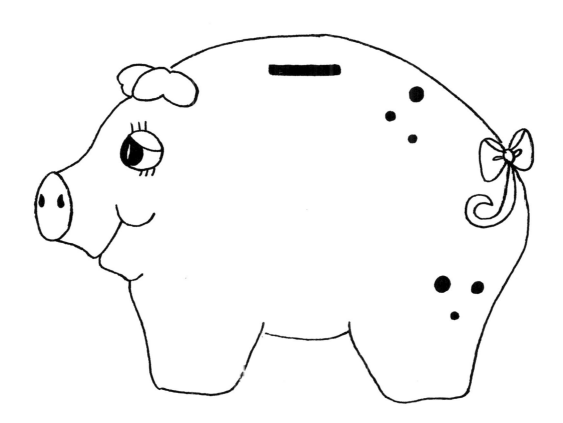

God loves a cheerful giver

"A joyful heart is good medicine,"

—*Proverbs 17:22*

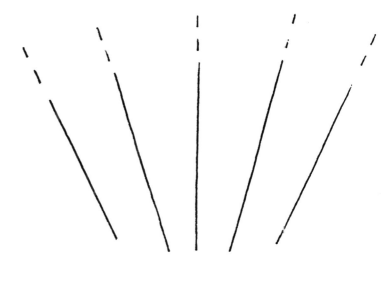

"I have directed you in the way of wisdom; I have led you in upright paths."

—*Proverbs 4:11*

walking
in the
foot prints
of Jesus

17

Did you forget to bring your Bible?

"Acquire wisdom! Acquire understanding! Do not forget, nor turn away from the words of my mouth."

—*Proverbs 4:5*

"Speaking to one another in psalms and hymns and spiritual songs, singing and making melody with your heart to the Lord;"

—*Ephesians 5:19*

let our hearts
be full of joy

The Beauty of God

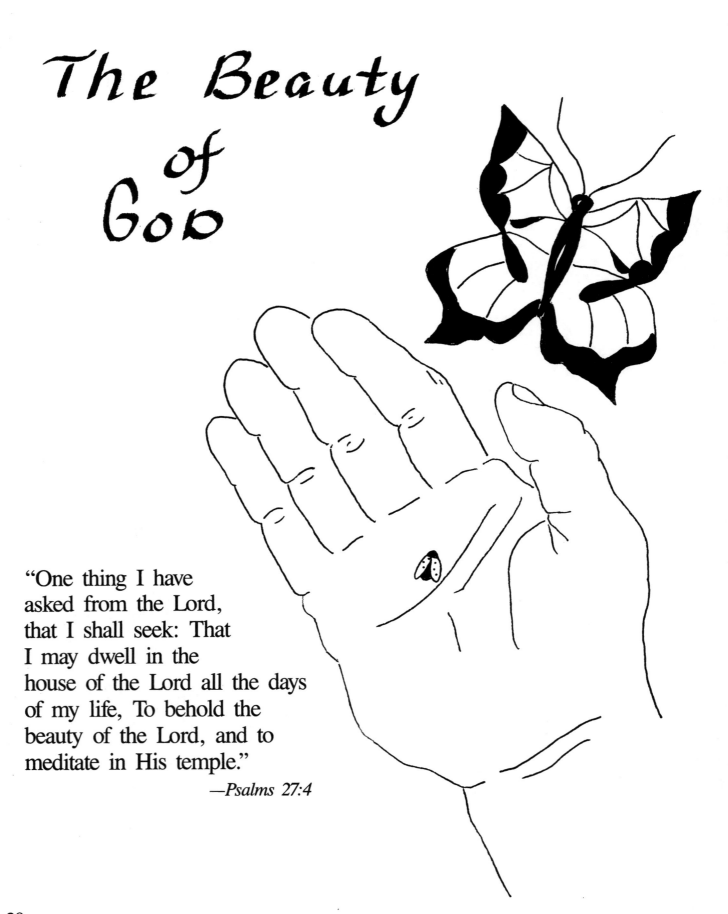

"One thing I have
asked from the Lord,
that I shall seek: That
I may dwell in the
house of the Lord all the days
of my life, To behold the
beauty of the Lord, and to
meditate in His temple."

—Psalms 27:4

20

you cannot be complete ... without

Christ!

"and in Him you have been made complete, and He is the head over all rule and authority;"

—*Colossians 2:10*

Partly Sunny or Partly Cloudy

How do you look at Life!

"in everything give thanks; for this is God's will for you in Christ Jesus."

—*1 Thessalonians 5:18*

Each day I'll do a golden deed

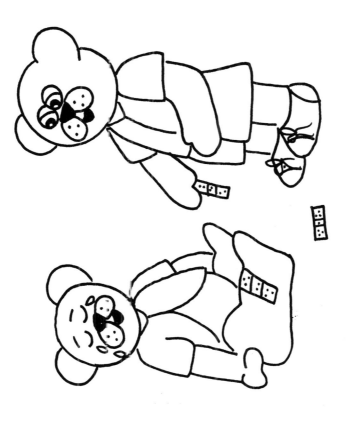

"Therefore, however you want people to treat you, so treat them, for this is the Law and the Prophets."

—Matthew 7:12

23

"so we, who are many, are one body in Christ, and individually members one of another."

—*Romans 12:5*

Tall

or

Small

God loves us all

We Thank thee, Lord

"always giving thanks for all things in the name of our Lord Jesus Christ to God, even the Father; . . ."

—*Ephesians 5:20*

"But I say to you, love your enemies, and pray for those who persecute you. . ."

—*Matthew 5:44*

Let us be quick
to hear &

Slow to Anger

"But let everyone be quick to hear, slow to speak and slow to anger;"

—*James 1:19*

"Therefore, to one who knows the right thing to do, and does not do it, to him it is sin."

—James 4:17

Watch out for the WEB of Sin

sin

don't let it trap you!

"And do not neglect doing good and sharing; for with such sacrifices God is pleased."

—*Hebrews 13:16*

Share God's Love...
tell someone you care!

The Best masterpiece ever painted is a SMILE !

"The lips of the righteous bring forth what is acceptable, . . ."

—*Proverbs 10:32*

"And He is before all things, and in Him all things hold together."

—Colossians 1:17

With out Christ ...
we fall apart

Don't get Caught up in Sin

"For if we go on sinning willfully after receiving the knowledge of the truth, there no longer remains a sacrifice for sins,"

—*Hebrews 10:26*

Life is fragile
handle with prayer

"pray without ceasing;"

—*1 Thessalonians 5:17*

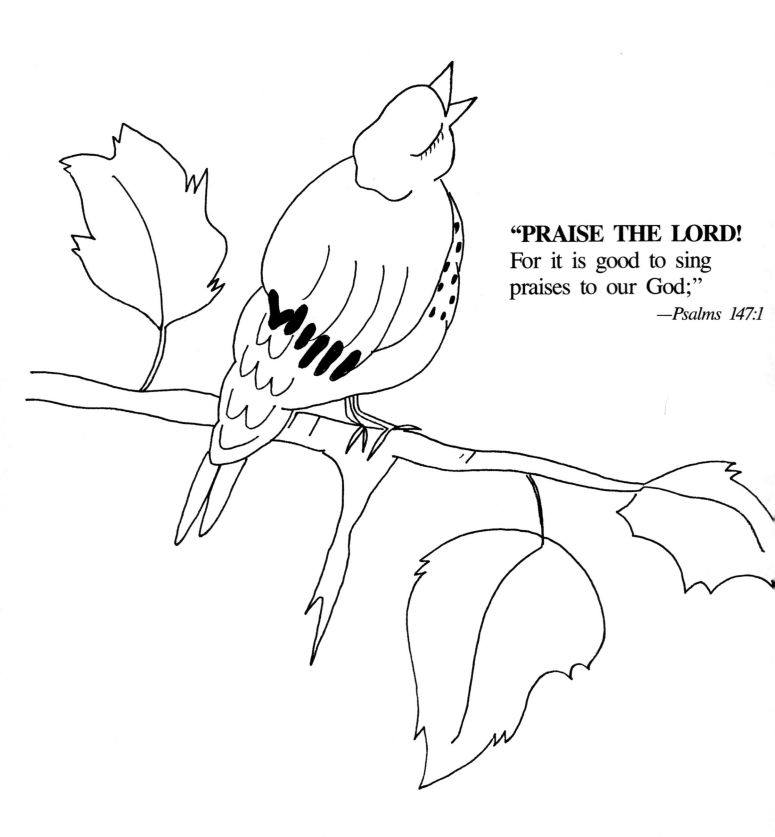

"PRAISE THE LORD!
For it is good to sing
praises to our God;"

—*Psalms 147:1*

"bearing with one another, and forgiving each other, whoever has a complaint against anyone; just as the Lord forgave you, so also should you."

—Colossians 3:13

"Bear" with us in our Class

Are you Sowing Seeds for God?

"Do not be deceived, God is not mocked; for whatever a man sows, this he will also reap."

—*Ephesians 6:7*

"How blessed are those who dwell in Thy house! They are ever praising Thee."

—*Psalms 84:4*

Bless our happy Home!

Are you following Jesus?

"I have no greater joy than this, to hear of my children walking in the truth."

—3 John 4

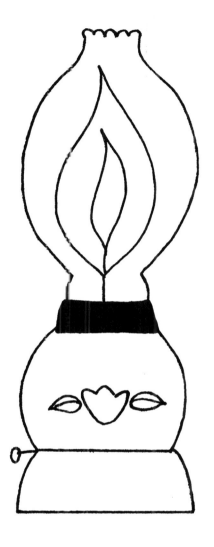

"For the commandment is a lamp, and the teaching is light;"
—*Proverbs 6:23*

The word of God will give us light!

"Let the words of my mouth and the meditation of my heart be acceptable in thy sight,"

—*Psalms 19:14*

"All scripture is inspired by God and profitable for teaching, for reproof, for correction, for training in righteousness;"

—*2 Timothy 3:16*

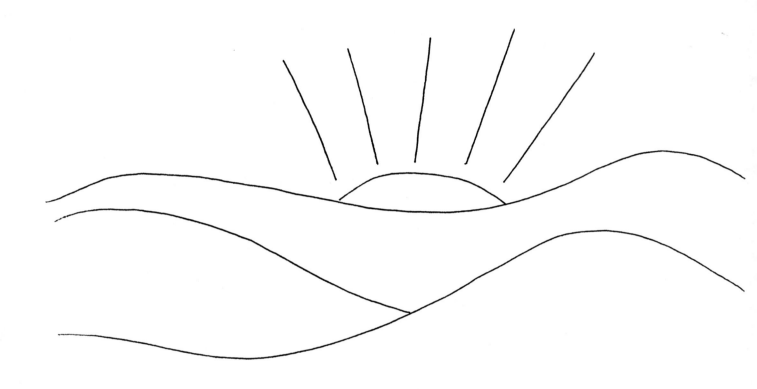

". . .do not let the sun go down on your anger,"

—*Ephesians 4:26*

Kind words are as sweet as honey

"Pleasant words are a honeycomb, sweet to the soul and healing to the bones."

—*Proverbs 16:24*

"The grass withers, the flower fades, but the word of our God stands forever."

—Isaiah 40:8

"I am the good shepherd; the good shepherd lays down His life for the sheep."

—*John 10:11*

Jesus is our Shepherd

"A joyful heart makes a cheerful face,"

—*Proverbs 15:13*

"To you has been given the mystery of the kingdom of God; but those who are outside get everything in parables,"

—*Matthew 4:11*

Goᴅ is the answer for all the questions

"Do you not know that
you are a temple of God,
and that the Spirit of God
dwells in you?"

—1 Corinthians 3:16

Can other's see Christ in you?

WALK
with
GOD

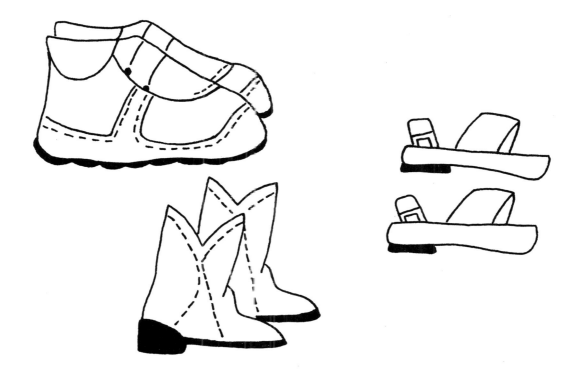

"for we walk by faith, not by sight—"

—2 Corinthians 5:7

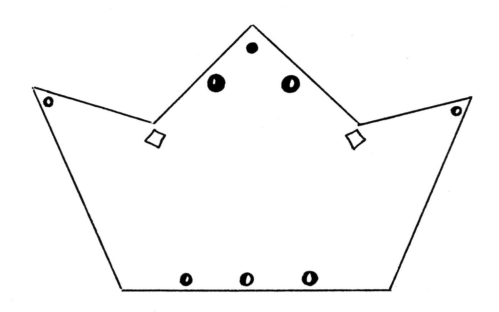

"Blessed is a man who perseveres under trial; for once he has been approved, he will receive the crown of life, which the Lord has promised to those who love Him."

—*James 1:12*

Will you receive "The Crown of life"?

Jesus is our Light

"For Thou dost light my lamp; The Lord my God illumines my darkness."

—*Psalms 18:28*

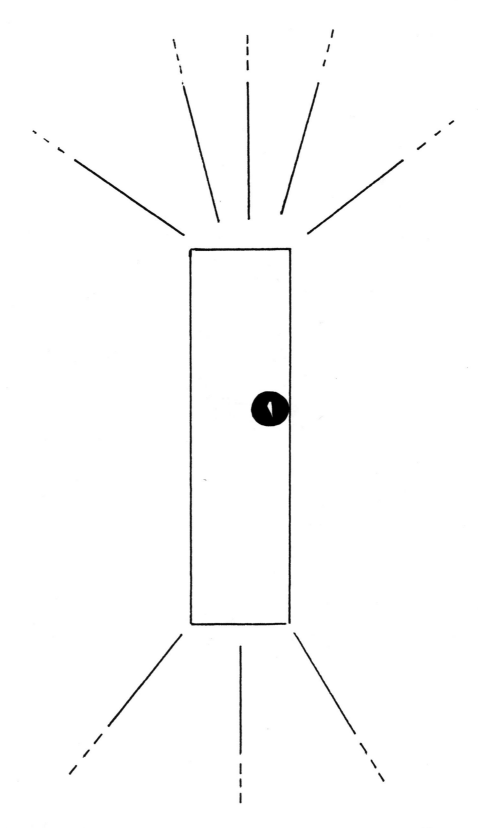

"Strive to enter by the narrow door; for many, I tell you, will
seek to enter and will not be able."

—*Luke 13:24*

"Suffer hardship with me, as a good soldier of Christ Jesus."

—*2 Timothy 2:3*

"For with thee is the fountain of life; In Thy light we see light."

—*Psalms 36:9*

54

"one God and Father of all who is over all and through all and in all."

—*Ephesians 4:6*

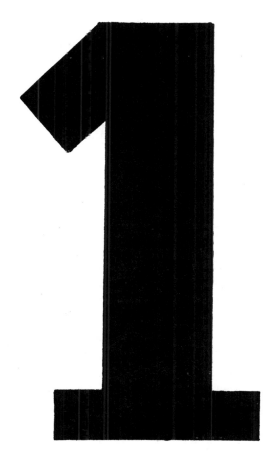

Be Wise
Study God's
Word

"How blessed is the man who finds wisdom, And the man who gains understanding."

—*Proverbs 3:13*

friends are a gift from God

"Beloved, let us love one another, for love is from God; and everyone who loves is born of God and knows God."

—1 John 4:7

"the Lord is King forever and ever;"

—*Psalms 10:16*

Jesus
is our Heavenly
King

"The mind of man plans his way, But the Lord directs his steps."

—*Proverbs 16:9*

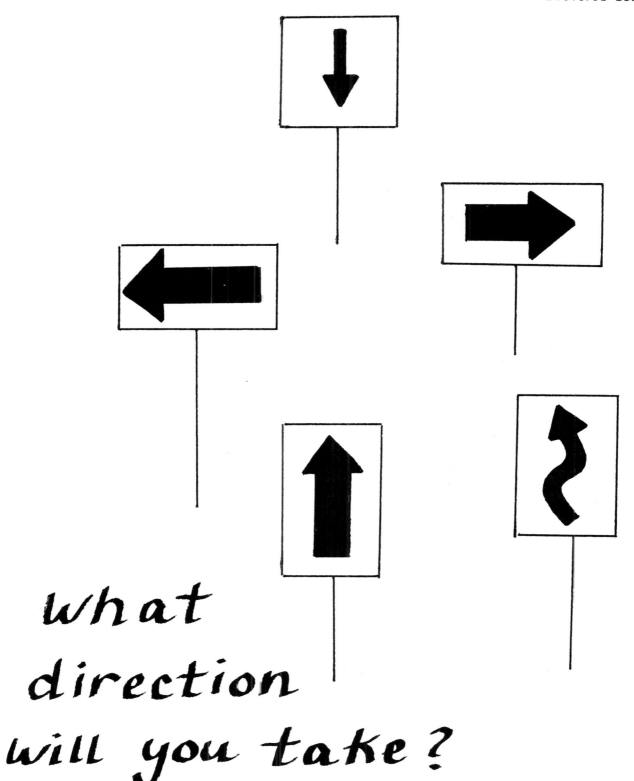

what
direction
will you take?

Treasure's on Earth -or- Treasure's in Heaven

"for where your treasure is, there will your heart be also."

—*Matthew 6:21*

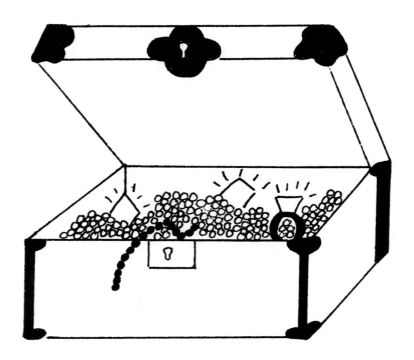

"And take the HELMET OF SALVATION, and the sword of the Spirit, which is the word of God."

—*Ephesians 6:17*

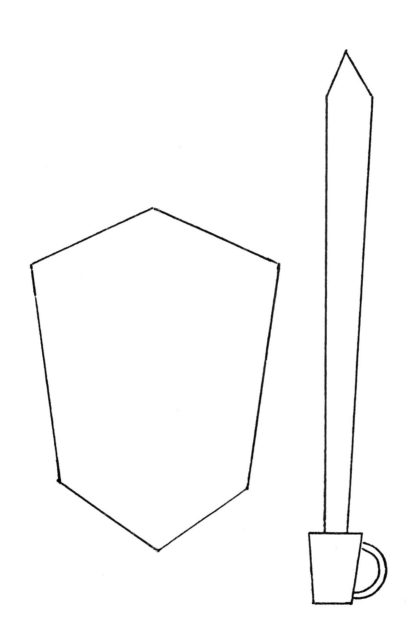

a mother's Love

a Blessing from God

"Her children rise up and bless her;"

—*Proverbs 31:28*

"But the fruit of the Spirit is love, joy, peace, patience, kindness, goodness, faithfulness, gentleness, self-control; against such things there is no law."

—*Galatians 5:22*

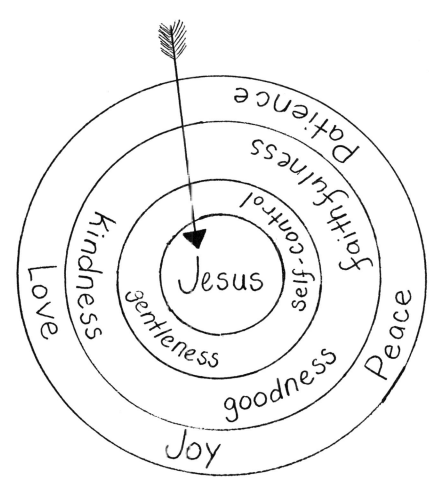

Aim for Jesus as the center of your life!

Count your Blessings!

"Behold, children are a gift of the Lord;"

—*Psalms 127:3*

"when you lie down, you will not be afraid; when you lie down, your sleep will be sweet."

—Proverbs 3:24

Goᴅ is with us

Bring your friends to Bible Class

"Let the little children alone, and do not hinder them from coming to Me; for the kingdom of heaven belongs to such as these."

—*Matthew 19:14*

"For the love of Christ controls us, having concluded this, that one died for all, therefore all died;"

—*2 Corinthians 5:14*

who has control of you?

"Be patient, therefore, brethren, until the coming of the Lord. Behold, the farmer waits for the precious produce of the soil, being patient about it, until it gets the early and late rains."

—*James 5:7*

will you be ready at harvest time?

I'm Popping up to welcome

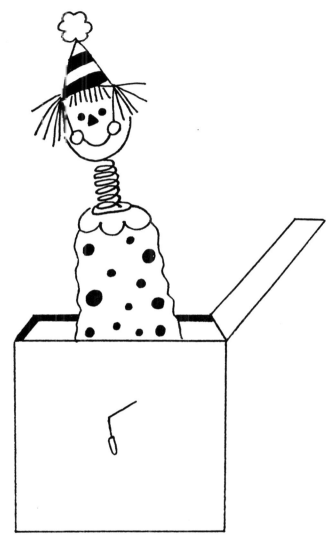

you to Bible Class

"Rejoice always;"

—2 Thessalonians 5:16

"Come to Me, all you who are weary and heavy-laden, and I will give you rest."

—Matthew 11:28

Are you carrying a heavy load?

"And whoever receives one such child in My name receives Me;"

—*Matthew 18:5*

"I can do all things through Him who strengthens me."

—Philippians 4:13

"All who are with me greet you. Greet those who love us in the faith."

—*Titus 3:15*

We are not "Lion" we are glad you came to Bible Class!

"Do you not know that those who run in a race all run, but only one receives the prize? Run in such a way that you may win."

—1 Corinthians 9:24

At the end of lives race will you be a winner?

"Every good thing bestowed and every perfect gift is from above, coming down from the Father of lights, with whom there is no variation, or shifting shadow."

—James 1:17

God gave us the gift of life!

"Repent, and let each of you be baptized in the name of Jesus Christ for the forgiveness of your sins; and you shall receive the gift of the Holy Spirit."

—*Acts 2:38*

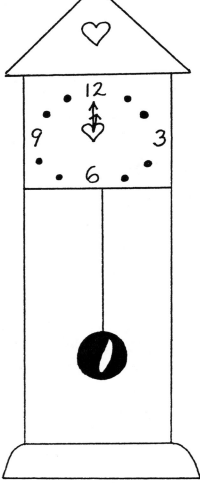

Don't wait until it is too late... Become a Christian Now!

Stop and study God's word!

Slow down listen and obey his commandments!

Go and tell others the good news!

"Go into all the world and preach the gospel to all creation."
—*Mark 16:15*

"Cast your burden upon the Lord, and he will sustain you; He will never allow the righteous to be shaken."

—*Psalms 55:22*

Lean on God he will support you!

"I am the way, and the truth, and the life; no one comes to the Father, but through me."

—*John 14:6*

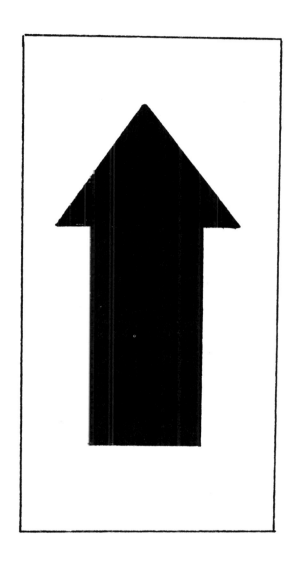

Jesus is the only way!

Do you measure up to God's Standards?

"For in the way you judge, you will be judged; and by your standard of measure, it will be measured to you."

—*Matthew 7:2*

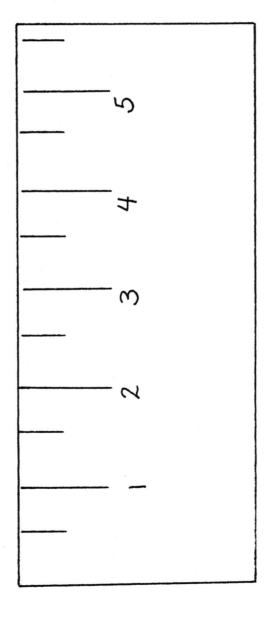

"And everyone who hears these words of Mine, and does not act upon them, will be like a foolish man, who built his house upon the sand."

—*Matthew 7:26*

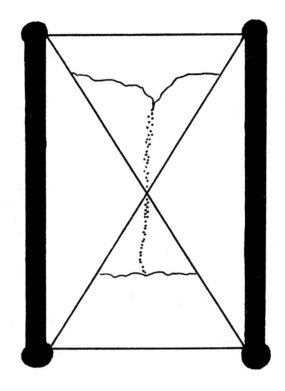

The hour is near...

Will you be ready?

"Therefore be on alert, for you do not know which day your Lord is coming."

—*Matthew 24:42*

Helping Other's

"do not merely look out for your own personal interests, but also for the interests of others."

—*Philippians 2:4*

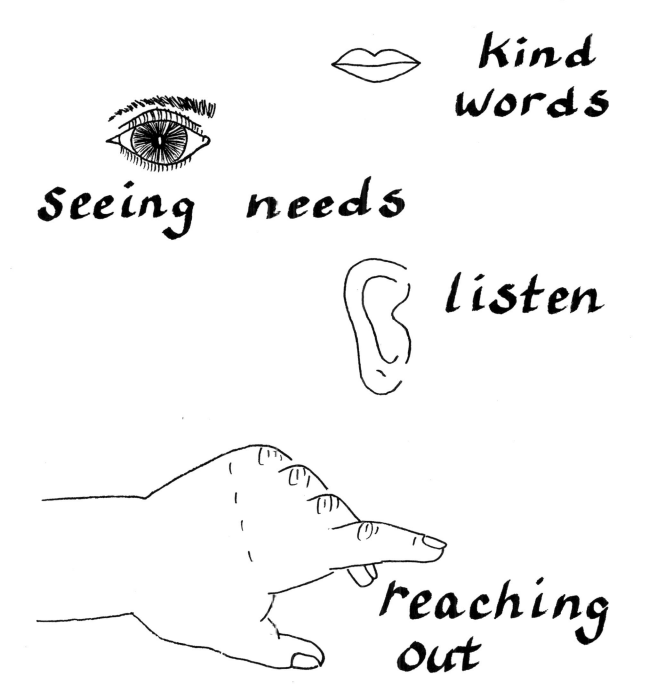

Kind words

Seeing needs

listen

reaching out

BRICKS

make a Strong house ... but only God can hold it together

"The wicked are overthrown and are no more, But the house of the righteous will stand."

—*Proverbs 12:7*

I'm hopping by to say...
I'm glad to see you here today!

"Until I come, give attention to the public reading of Scripture, to exhortation and teaching."

—1 Timothy 4:13

Season's pass but God never changes

"Jesus Christ is the same yesterday and today, yes and forever."
—*Hebrews 13:8*

"REJOICE in the Lord always; again I will say, REJOICE!"

—*Philippians 4:4*

Will your Anchor hold during the rocky waves of life?

"This hope we have as an anchor of the soul, a hope both sure and steadfast and one which enters within the veil,"

—*Hebrews 6:19*

FOR PROPER USE ONLY!

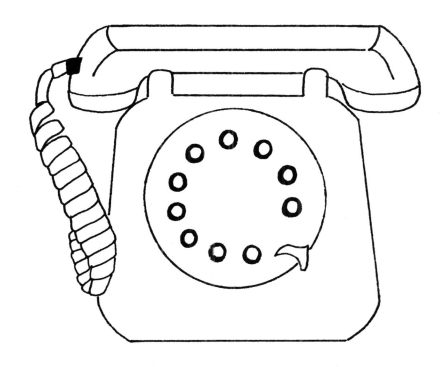

"But avoid wordly and empty chatter, for it will lead to further ungodliness, . . ."

—2 Timothy 2:16

Christian's are united in God's Love

"BEHOLD, how good and how pleasant it is for brothers to dwell together in unity!"

—*Psalms 133:1*

"Thou didst shed abroad a plentiful rain, O God;"

—Psalms 68:9

Is the Bible the foundation of your home?

"For no man can lay a foundation other than the one which is laid, which is Jesus Christ."

—1 Corinthians 3:11

Jesus will help you "IRON" out your problems!

"Therefore do not be anxious for tomorrow; for tomorrow will care for itself. Each day has enough trouble of its own."

—*Matthew 6:34*

We are aiming high!

"Thy lovingkindness, O Lord, extends to the heavens, Thy faithfulness reaches to the skies."

—*Psalms 36:5*

"I will give you the keys of the kingdom of heaven; . . ."

—*Matthew 16:19*

You cannot hide from God

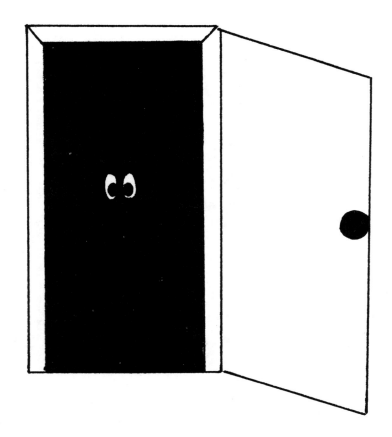

"For nothing is hidden, except to be revealed; nor has anything been secret, but that it should come to light."

—Mark 4:22

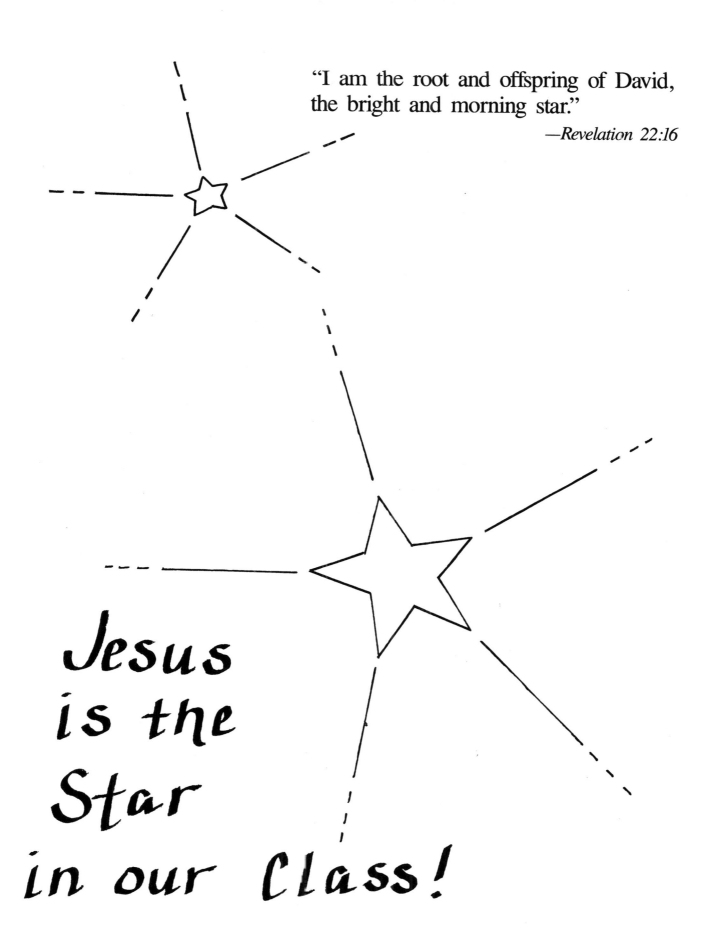

"I am the root and offspring of David, the bright and morning star."

—*Revelation 22:16*

Jesus
is the
Star
in our Class!

". . .The Lord is my helper, I will not be afraid."

—*Hebrews 13:6*

Are you hiding behind a Wall of doubts and fears?

"Whoever then humbles himself as this child, he is the greatest in the kingdom of heaven."

—*Matthew 18:4*

"make my joy complete by being of the same mind, maintaining the same love, united in spirit, intent on one purpose."

—*Philippians 2:2*

Christians are Linked together with God's love

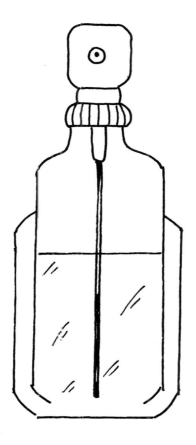

"Oil and perfume make the heart glad, So a man's counsel is sweet to his friend."

—*Proverbs 27:9*

Instructions for Bulletin Board Ideas

1. The clock can be enlarged on white board or paper, cut out black paper for the rim. You can draw the face on, or use pipe cleaners. Pipe cleaners can also be used for the arms and legs. The road sign can be cut from brown paper or cardboard. This can be enlarged and colored in.

2. These little friends can be enlarged and colored in, or you can cut them out of colored paper. The dog can be cut from light brown paper with black spots, and the cat can be out of white or gray. You can use a real rug or make one out of material and glue yarn on for the fringe.

3. This bright clown will brighten up any classroom. The clown can be enlarged and colored in, or you can enlarge him and trace onto paper. The suit can be from bright paper with different colored dots. The ruffles on the suit can be cut out of material or paper, you could also use lace. The clowns eyes can be cut out of paper or you could use the large plastic eyes found at craft stores. The nose and cheeks can be colored in or cut out of red or pink paper. The clowns face can be cut from cream colored paper, or you can color it. For the hair you can cut strips of paper or pieces of yarn. The balls can be cut from bright colored paper, or you could even use balloons.

4. This apple tree is great enlarged and colored in, or cut it out of paper. The leaves can be cut from green paper or felt. The apples are cut from bright red paper or felt. Another idea is to use wood-grain contact paper for the tree trunk. This can also be used for an attendance chart. The apples can represent the times the student was in bible class.

5. This little book worm can be enlarged onto bright green paper, or he can be enlarged and colored in. The bible can be cut out of paper or you could even use a small childrens bible. The glasses can be made from pipe cleaners. The eyes are cut from paper, or you can use the large plastic eyes.

6. The mother and baby duck can be cut from yellow felt or enlarged onto yellow paper. The duck's bill and feet are from orange felt or orange paper. The hearts can be cut out of red paper or felt. Real ribbon tied around the neck and placed in the baby duck's mouth really gives this a great touch.

7. The cup can be from any light colored board or paper. The red hearts really are pretty when cut from red satin. You could also use red cellophane or wrapping paper.

8. This bright sun is great for any age. This can be enlarged onto yellow paper and cut out. The eyes can be cut out of paper or you can use the large plastic eyes. The mouth and nose can be made from pipe cleaners.

9. The hearts can be enlarged onto red or white paper. You can cut out the letters from black paper or you could even use pipe cleaners to form the letters. Another way would be to use red material and write the words on the hearts with glue, then sprinkle glitter on the glue.

10. This tree is nice if you enlarge the pattern on paper and then cut the tree trunk out of wood-grain contact paper. The leaves can be out of green paper or felt. The hearts are pretty cut from red satin or felt. You can also enlarge this onto white paper and color it in.

11. This is especially good for the fall. This can be enlarged and colored in, or you can make a pattern and cut the bear from felt or even fur. The clothes can be cut from material. The tree trunk looks good cut out of wood-grain contact paper. You can cut the leaves out of different colored paper, or you can buy artificial leaves at a craft store or florist.

12. The doors are best when cut from heavy white paper or poster board. The letters can be cut from black paper (for the "darkness of sin") and silver, gold, or bright yellow (for the "LIGHT OF JESUS". The light rays could be made from cardboard strips covered in foil or gold glitter.

13. The doghouse and friends can be enlarged and colored in or traced onto colored paper. The dogs can be from different shades of brown. You can cut eyes out of paper or use the large plastic eyes. The dogs spots can be painted on or cut from black paper. The house is enlarged and traced onto red paper with black for the trim.

14. The flowers can be artificial flowers glued onto a light blue background. You can use pipe cleaners to form the letters. The flowers also look good, cut from different colored tissue paper. The stems and leaves can be from felt, or you can use pipe cleaners for the stems and cut the leaves from felt. The little bees can be made from felt or you can buy fuzzy bees at a craft store.

15. This piggy bank is good for adult classes. The pig can be cut from pink felt or wrapping paper. You can use a large plastic eye or make one cut of paper. The tail can be a pipe cleaner or yarn. You can also tie a real ribbon around the tail.

16. This is a good idea for any age. The heart can be enlarged onto red paper or felt. The eyes can be cut from paper or you can glue large plastic eyes on. The nose and mouth can be made from pipe cleaners and the cheeks out of bright pink paper or felt.

17. The footsteps can be cut from heavy white paper or poster board. The rays of light can be strips of poster board covered in foil or glitter. You can also write the students names on the footprints. Underneath the footprints you could write "My class is following the steps of Jesus".

18. They say an elephant never forgets! This is especially good for a teen-age class room. Enlarge this onto gray wrapping paper or you could use white and color it in. The church, tree and bushes can be colored in. You could also cut the windows out of the church and glue in colored cellophane behind them.

19. This heart can be enlarged onto red paper or poster board. The musical notes can be cut out of black paper or pipe cleaners.

20. This hand is best enlarged onto white paper and drawn in with black marker. The little bug can be cut out of red felt. You can either use an artificial butterfly or make one out of tissue paper.

21. This idea is best if enlarged onto white paper and the semi-circle is drawn in with a heavy thick marker. The circle should be about 1 inch thick.

22. This is pretty when you use a light blue paper for the background. The sun and clouds can be cut out of yellow felt for the sun and the clouds can be made out of poly-fiber-fill or cotton.

23. These bears can be enlarged onto white paper and colored in or make a pattern and cut them out of brown felt or paper. You could even use material for the clothes. Be sure to use real Band-aids to give this a special touch.

24. The giraffe can be enlarged onto yellow paper. You can cut out spots from black paper or color in. The hair, and eyelashes can be out of pipe cleaners. You can cut the antennas out of yellow paper or use yellow pipe cleaners. The little mouse can be cut out of brown paper or light gray. The giraffes eyes can be out of paper or you can use the large plastic eyes.

25. The bears can be enlarged onto white paper and colored in, or you can cut them out of brown paper. You can make the dress out of material with lace for the trim. The shoes are out of black paper. The blanket can be a piece of material or even an old tablecloth.

26. This cat and friends can be enlarged onto a light background and colored in or you can trace them onto paper. The cat can be gray or even black. The little birds are all different colors, and the mouse is light brown or gray. The cats eyes are cut from yellow paper with black centers.

27. The rabbit is enlarged onto white paper. You can use the large plastic eyes or cut some out of paper. The turtle is cut out of light green paper for the body and a darker green for the shell. The turtles shell is outlined in black. You can cut the eyes from paper or glue on plastic eyes. The shell could also be cut from different shades of green and layered on.

28. The spider web is best if made from yarn or string. You can staple this onto a light gray or blue background. The spider can be a plastic one from a toy store or make one out of pipe cleaners. The words can also be formed out of pipe cleaners.

29. The mailbox can be enlarged onto white paper and colored in. You can also make a pattern and cut the mailbox out of gray paper. The pole can be cut from wood-grain contact paper. The fence can be out of popsicle sticks with string glued on them. The bird can be out of red or blue felt.

30. This little artist can be enlarged onto paper and colored in or a pattern can be made. The bear can be made out of brown paper or felt. The coat can be out of material, you can make the hat out of black felt. The bear's bow can be a scarf or ribbon. The paint palette can be made from cardboard. You can use a real paint brush and dabs of paint on the palette.

31. This can be enlarged on white poster board actually cut out and glued backed together or enlarged and colored in. You could even use a real puzzle.

32. The fish can be enlarged onto green paper and cut out. The fish scales should be layered. Cut the eyes out of paper. You could also use small styrofoam balls cut in half with a black dot glued on. The fish hook can be a string with a bent paper clip. (For precaution you might not want to use a real fish hook)

33. This can be enlarged and colored in or you can get a large styrofoam ball or egg shaped styrofoam at a craft store. Cut the styrofoam into and then glue a chicks head made out of felt or paper. You can use black buttons, sequins or dots for the eyes.

34. This is a real pretty poster. The bird can be enlarged and colored in with bright markers or crayons. You could also trace it onto red or blue paper and cut out. The branch could be made from wood-grain contact paper. The leaves can be made out of green paper or felt.

35. This bear can be enlarged and cut out of brown paper or felt. The eyes can be cut out or you can use large plastic eyes. The honey pot can be made from paper. The bow can be cut out of paper or you can use ribbon. The balloon can be a real one or made from paper. The bee can be cut out of felt. You could also use a fuzzy bee from a craft store.

36. This is a good spring bulletin board. The sticks can be real sticks or even popsicle sticks. The cards are approx. 6 x 6 cards cut from poster board. You can use yarn for the weeds or paper.

37. This is also great for spring or summer. The bird house is best when you enlarge it onto red poster board and cut out. The hole in the center should be cut out with black or brown in the background. The birds can be cut from felt or paper. The beaks and feet can be cut out of yellow, orange or gold felt. Inside the house put pieces of yellow yarn or string. The pole can be a stick or cardboard covered in wood-grain contact paper.

38. This family can be enlarged and colored in or cut from yellow paper. The bills and webbed feet can be cut out of orange felt. The sign can be cardboard covered in wood-grain contact paper. You could also make the sign from cardboard and paint the word and arrow on it. The weeds can be yarn or pieces of string.

39. The lamp can be enlarged onto white paper and colored in. This would make a good poster also. You can cut the base of the lamp from gold or silver wrapping paper. Cut out the black trim and flower and then glue on. The bulb can be made from clear cellophane with the flame made out of yellow paper.

40. These talkative hens can be enlarged and colored in or trace it onto brown paper and cut out. You can layer the pieces of paper to make it look like feathers. The head can be cut from yellow paper. The eyes can be large plastic eyes or cut eyes out of paper. The nests can be yarn or string cut up and glued onto the background.

41. This can be enlarged onto paper and colored in or enlarge it onto colored paper and cut out. The trim around the blackboard can be any light color. The bear can be cut out of brown felt or paper. The bears vest and pants can be cut out of material. You can attach real pieces of chalk to his paw. The words can be painted on.

42. This is best when enlarged onto different shades of green or brown paper, for the hills, and yellow for the sun. This can be glued onto a light gray or blue background.

43. The honey pot can be enlarged onto white paper for a pattern and then cut out brown paper or felt for the pot. The honey can be cut from yellow plastic, felt cellophane or paper. Make a bee out of felt or use a fuzzy bee.

44. The flowers can be artificial flowers bent so they look like they are drooping or cut them out of paper. The grass can be from light green and yellow paper or yarn.

45. A pattern can be enlarged for the sheep. After you have made the pattern cut the sheep out of white felt, flannel, or quilt batting. You could also enlarge this onto white poster board and glue cotton on for the body and black felt for the face and feet.

46. This bear is good when enlarged onto brown paper and cut out. You could also make a pattern and cut him out of fur or felt. The heart can be cut out of red felt or satin. You can make the faces out of felt. The bunny shoes can be cut out or pink flannel or fleece.

47. This is a good poster. Enlarge it and color it in with a black marker. This idea could also be enlarged onto paper and cut out.

48. This little duck can be enlarged and colored in or make pattern and cut her out of yellow felt. The apron can be from material. The eyes can be cut out of paper. The mirror is cardboard covered in foil. The reflection can be on the foil, or cut one out of paper and glue it on.

49. The shoes can be enlarged onto different colored paper and cut out. This can be glued onto a light background with the words cut out and glued on.

50. This crown looks best when a pattern is enlarged and then the crown is cut out of cardboard and covered with foil. The jewels can be real pieces of jewelry or sequins glued on.

51. This can be enlarged onto white paper or board. You can also make a pattern for it and cut the face and paws from brown felt or paper. The pajamas can be out of blue flannel. You could use a sock or a piece of flannel or felt for the hat. The candle can be out of red paper. You can cut the candle holder out of gold or silver wrapping paper. The flame can be yellow cellophane or yellow paper.

52. This door is best when a pattern is enlarged and the door is cut out of white poster board or cardboard. You can then cover it with gold or silver wrapping paper. The light rays can be gold pipe cleaners or cardboard strips covered in foil.

53. The soldier is good for kindergarten up to young adult classes. The soldier can be enlarged and colored in. You could also make a pattern and cut the clothes out of red and blue material. The face can be colored in with a peach crayon or chalk, on white paper. The hair, belt, and boots, can be painted on or cut from black paper. You can use a real feather or cut one out of yellow paper. The medal can be made from cardboard covered in foil.

54. The fountain can be enlarged onto white poster board and outlined in black or blue. The water can be a piece of foil cut in an oval shape and glued onto the fountain. The birds can be colored onto the white poster or cut out of paper or felt. This can all be cut out and glued onto a light background.

55. The "1" can be enlarged onto white poster board and drawn in with black marker. This is good for kindergarten and up.

56. The owl and branch can be enlarged onto brown paper and cut out. The leaves can be out of green felt. The owls eyes can be cut out of paper. The feathers of the owl can be cut out of gold felt and then glued onto the brown paper. The owl's beak and claws are made out of yellow paper.

57. These friends can be enlarged and colored on white paper. You can also make a pattern and cut the bear from brown felt or paper. The duck can be out of yellow paper or felt. The wings should be cut out separately. The duck's bill and feet are cut from orange paper. The bow can be a real ribbon or even a large bow-tie. The little bear can be out of paper or felt.

58. This crown is best if a pattern is enlarged onto cardboard and then covered in foil or gold wrapping paper. You can glue pieces of jewelry or sequins onto the crown.

59. This is a good poster or it can be enlarged and each sign cut out separately and glued on a light blue background. You can either cut the arrows out of black paper or paint them onto white poster board. The signs should be cut in all different size rectangles. The poles could be sticks, pipe cleaners or cardboard cut in strips.

60. This is a good poster or bulletin board for adult classes. The treasure chest can be enlarged onto white paper and colored in. You can also cut a chest from silver wrapping paper, trimmed in black paper. The coins and jewels can either be real or use large sequins.

61. This is good enlarged onto white poster board and covered in foil or silver wrapping paper.

62. This is good for cradle-roll or the nursery. The mother bear can be enlarged onto brown paper, for the face and paws, the little bears face can also be cut from the brown paper. The blanket can be any color of flannel, you could also use a real baby blanket. The mother's dress can be out of paper with the hearts glued on, or you could use any kind of fabric. The shoes can be cut out of felt, and the hat cut from felt or material.

63. This makes a excellent poster. The target can be enlarged and colored in on white poster board. The arrow can be drawn in. For this idea you could also cut it out of yellow paper with a red center. The words could be written on. You can also use a real arrow for this, but be sure to use one with a dull tip.

64. This is a good poster for cradle-roll, nursery, or toddlers. The rabbits can be enlarged onto white paper. The faces, hands and feet can be cut out. You can cut the clothes out of different pieces of material or paper. If you cut the clothes out of fabric use buttons, and lace for a realistic look.

65. This sleeping bear is really good for toddler up to junior classes. The bears and blanket can be enlarged and colored in or make a pattern and cut out. The bear really looks best if cut out of brown felt. The pillow can be cut out of flannel and the blanket could be a real baby blanket or pieces of flannel sewed together. The little bear is also cute cut out of felt.

66. These friends are great for any age, but especially school age. The wagon and friends can be enlarged and cut out of paper. Red paper for the wagon, brown for the bear and yellow for the ducks. The duck's bills are out of orange paper, and the bows can be real ribbon. The big bear can be enlarged on brown paper and cut out. The vest can be out of felt or material. The wagons wheels can be cardboard painted black.

67. This is good enlarged and colored in. You can also cut it out in separate pieces. The head, shirt and pants out of paper. The shoes out of black paper or felt. Glue this onto a background and glue the string to the back of the puppet. Don't glue down the puppet all the way so it will look loose.

68. The farmer can be enlarged and colored in. You can also make a pattern and cut his overalls out of old jeans or material. The shirt out of red material. The hat can be out of burlap. The hoe can be out of cardboard. The farmers face and hair can be on white board that you color or paint. The plants can be pieces of yarn and felt. This is good for spring and summer.

69. A good poster or bulletin board for children. The box can be cut out of cardboard. The puppet can be made out of yarn, a styrofoam ball, and material. The head is a medium styrofoam ball. You can glue eyes, nose and mouth on. The hair can be pieces of yarn or pipe cleaners. The suit can be material glued to cardboard. The hat can be a cone shaped drinking cup, or a piece of paper cut out. The ball on the hat can be a cotton ball.

70. The ants can be enlarged onto white paper and colored in. This can also be cut out of paper. The ant can be out of black paper with red heads. The arms, legs, and antenna's can be out of pipe cleaners. The weeds can be out of pieces of yarn. The load the ant is carrying could be a piece of foil or paper crumbled up.

71. These bears can be enlarged onto brown paper for the hands and faces. The dress and suit can be out of paper or material. The balloons can be real balloons or they can be made out of paper or material.

72. This bear can be enlarged onto brown paper and cut out. The shirt and shorts out of red and blue or yellow and green. The weight can be a cardboard strip with two black balloons attached. You could also use cardboard painted black.

73. The lion can be enlarged and then cut out of brown and yellow paper or felt. The body can be out of yellow with a brown mane. The eyes can be large plastic eyes or cut them out of paper. The mane could also be yarn.

74. This is a good poster or bulletin board. The trophy can be enlarged onto silver or gold wrapping paper. The words could be written in black marker.

75. The present can be enlarged onto cardboard and then covered with real wrapping paper. You can cut a bow from paper or use real ribbon.

76. The clock can be enlarged onto brown paper and cut out. The clocks face can be white paper with the numbers and dots drawn in with a black marker. The hearts can be cut from red paper or felt.

77. This is best when enlarged onto yellow or white poster board. The circles can be cut out with red, yellow and green cellophane glued in the holes. This could also be traced onto cardboard and covered in silver wrapping paper.

78. This is a good poster for adults. The face can be drawn with a black marker. You could also color the face in.

79. This can be enlarged onto white poster board and the arrow painted in or cut out of black paper separately.

80. This ruler can be enlarged onto yellow poster board and the numbers and lines drawn in with black marker.

81. This is a good poster for adults. This can be enlarged onto white poster board and drawn with a black marker. The pail and shovel can be cut out of paper or colored in. You can also glue salt or sand to this.

82. This can be enlarged and a pattern cut. The glass part can be made out of clear plastic, cut in triangles. The two poles can be cardboard strips painted or colored black. Glue the triangles and poles together as pictured. Before you attach this to a background dripple on glue to make it stream down like the sand, then sprinkle on glitter. After the glitter is dry attach the hour glass to the background.

83. This can be a poster or bulletin board. Each of these can be enlarged and cut out of paper. This can be enlarged and colored in.

84. The word bricks can be enlarged and cut out of red paper. The roof out of black paper, and the bricks on the house out of gray, brown, or red. The door and windows can be cut from black paper.

85. The frog and lily pad are enlarged onto green paper. The frog needs to be a darker shade. The eyes can be the large plastic eyes or a styrofoam ball cut in half. The cat-tails can be out of gold felt and green pipe cleaners. The dragon-fly can be out of paper or a pipe cleaner and tissue paper.

86. This can be enlarged and colored in. The seasons can also be cut out of paper and glued onto blue background. The snowman can be out of white flannel or felt. The raindrops can be blue cellophane, the sun can be yellow cellophane. The seasons can be glued to the background with thin strips of silver paper cut for the bars of the window. You could also attach the scenes then place clear plastic or clear contact paper over them, divide the seasons with strips of paper.

87. This happy bird can be enlarged onto red, blue or yellow paper, and his beak and feet can be out of orange paper.

88. These little sailors can be enlarged and cut out of yellow paper. The hats can be out of white paper or material. The boat can be out of red paper. The waves are cut out of different shades of blue paper glued down on a light blue background. The fish are cut out of green paper. The anchor can be cardboard colored or painted black. The string can be yarn or even real fishing line.

89. This is good enlarged onto any color paper. The cord can even be from an old phone. You can also curl pipe cleaners or ribbon. The phone dial can be out of cardboard covered in the same color of paper as the phone. You can attach the dial with a paper fastener in the center so it will turn.

90. This is really cute when you cut them out of white paper and attach to a background. The hearts can be cut out of red paper or satin. The shoes and hair can be colored in.

91. This is a good poster or enlarged and cut out of yellow paper. The bills and feet are out of orange, the umbrella can be any color. The little duck's boots are cut out of red paper. The raindrops can be out of shades of blue paper. The eyes can be plastic eyes or cut from paper.

92. This house and bible can be enlarged and cut out. The bible can be cut out of white poster board with black trim. The house can be cut out of red paper with a brown roof, the windows can be white, yellow or they can even be cut out with cellophane glued on.

93. The iron can be enlarged and cut out of silver wrapping paper with a black trim. The cord can be black yarn or an old extension cord.

94. The kite and clouds can be enlarged and colored in. You can also make a kite out of tissue paper, and you can attach string to it. The clouds can be made out of cotton, and the sun rays can be out of foil.

95. The keys can be enlarged onto poster board and cut out. After you have cut them out you can cover them with foil or silver wrapping paper. The words can be written on or cut out of black paper and glued on.

96. This is a good poster or bulletin board. You can enlarge it and color it in or make the door frame out of wood-grain contact paper and use black paper for the inside. The eyes can be the large plastic eyes or cut them out of paper.

97. These stars can be enlarged onto white board and cut out. You can then cover them with foil or glitter.

98. This is great for adult classes. The bricks can be enlarged onto paper and colored in or you can enlarge it onto brown or red paper and cut out. The man can be colored onto the background or also cut out of paper. The bricks could also be small boxes or pieces of styrofoam covered in paper.

99. This is really a good poster for a children's bible class. This can be enlarged and colored in. The bear can also be cut out of brown paper for the face. The hat and pajamas can be out of flannel. The window scene is black paper with a moon glued onto it. The curtains can be out of material or use real ones. The bed can be out of paper. You could also use cardboard for the bed frame and material for the quilt.

100. This is best when the heart is made out of paper clips chained together or pipe cleaners. You could also make paper chains and form them in the shape of the heart.

101. This is a good poster or bulletin board. The bottle can be drawn on any color of paper or you can draw it on white paper and outline the bottle in black. The perfume could be colored in with yellow or pink.